TORU TAKEMITSU
LES YEUX CLOS II

for piano

SJ 1056

 SCHOTT

Mainz · London · New York · Tokyo

ピアノのための《閉じた眼II》は、ピーター・ゼルキンの委嘱により作曲され、1989年11月11日にニューヨークで初演された。

演奏時間——7分

"Les yeux clos II" was commissioned by Peter Serkin, who premiered it on November 11, 1989, in New York.

Duration: 7 minutes

This piece requires a piano with three pedals.

R	right (damper)
M	middle (sostenuto)
L	left (soft)
◢	rallenrando
◢	accelerando

to Peter Serkin

Les yeux clos II

for piano

Toru Takemitsu

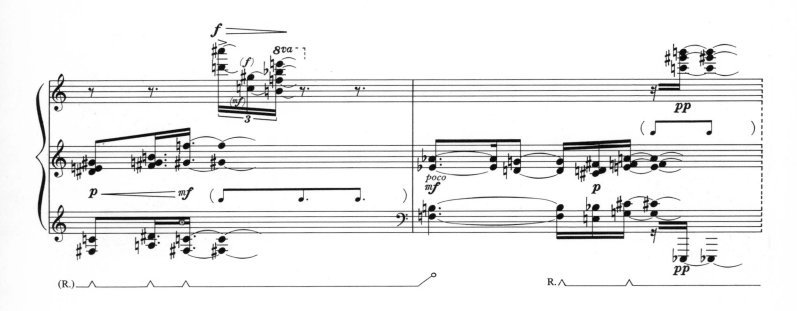

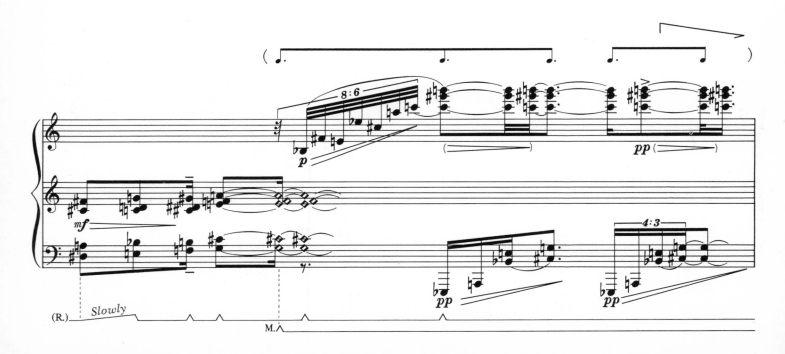

con ped. ad lib.

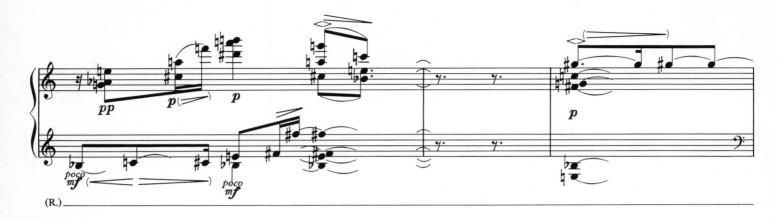

(R.)

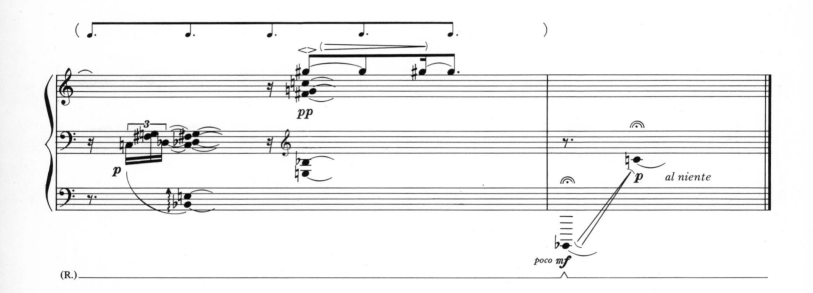

(R.)

武満徹《閉じた眼 II》　　　　　　　　●

初版発行—————————————————————————————1990年5月25日
第2版第1刷②————————————————————————1990年11月25日
発行—————————————————————————————日本ショット株式会社
———————————————————————————————東京都千代田区飯田橋3-4-3-301 〒102
———————————————————————————————(03) 263-6530
———————————————————————————————ISBN4-89066-356-8